Grapes Indoors and Out

ARTHUR TURNER AND HARRY BAKER
With Revisions by RAY WAITE
(RHS Garden, Wisley)

LONDON
The Royal Horticultural Society
Revised 1983

Contents

Photographs; Harry Baker, Audrey Brooks, Harry Smith Collection

1. Vines under glass

Up to the start of the last war vines were grown in special greenhouses, on their own. The vineries were divided by partitions to allow cultivation of early, mid-season and late fruiting cultivars which needed different conditions of heat.

After the war the days of the specialised vinery were ended and few people grew vines under glass. In the last two decades, however, interest has re-awakened and now more people are finding that they can grow a worthwhile crop of grapes in the roof space above the other plants in even a relatively small greenhouse.

The limiting factor in a small greenhouse is its height, but the current fashion in amateur greenhouses is for a greater height to the eaves so this factor is becoming less of a problem. If there is choice of structure, a south-facing lean-to is the most suitable as the roof rises across the whole width of the house and in addition the rear wall collects a reserve of heat on a sunny day which is released into the house at night.

Preparation for planting

A vine may be planted outside the greenhouse in a border with the main stem (called the rod) led into the greenhouse through a hole cut low down in the wall, or planted in an inside border either with the roots left free to wander outside or with the roots restricted in some form of large trough buried in the border. They can, if desired, be grown in a tub or some other large container, and in that case the length of the rod should be limited to 6 or 8 feet (1.8 to 2.1m) and the crop weight will also have to be restricted. Such a restricted root run is needed when there is any risk of the roots growing into areas where they might become waterlogged in winter or suffer damage in any way.

Growing a vine in an outside border can reduce the risk of over or under watering, and less frequent attention will be required, as in the average summer natural rainfall will meet much of the demand. If there is the fear of too much water a polythene sheet can be laid down to direct it away from the root area. For a plant in an outside border, provided the soil is well drained and fertile then double digging with the incorporation of some well rotted manure, bonfire ash and a general fertilizer, is all that is required to prepare the soil before planting.

With the roots in a border inside the greenhouse the grower has more control—success or failure depends on his or her knowledge and judgement. A vine in an inside border has the advantage of warmer soil in early spring. This is not such a critical factor if the vines are being started into growth naturally in March but is of some importance if the vines are started with artificial heat in February when the soil outside is often cold and wet. For an inside border, particularly if the roots are to be restricted, the soil should be open and porous in texture, capable of remaining that way for many years, yet able to hold reasonable reserves of plant food. A soil mixture made up to approximately the John Innes No 3 Potting Compost recipe (i.e. 7 parts of loam, 3 parts of peat, 2 parts of coarse sand, plus (per bushel) 12 oz of J.I. base fertilizer and $2\frac{1}{4}$ oz of ground chalk) will provide a very satisfactory medium. Substitute coarse grit for the sand and if wood ash from the bonfire containing charcoal is available this can also be included in the mixture.

Good drainage is of the utmost importance. If your soil is naturally well drained then there may be no need to make special arrangements but should there be any doubt on the point then a line of land drain-pipes, about 4 inches (10cm) in diameter, should be laid across the area with an even fall toward a ditch, surface water drain or a soakaway prepared by digging a very deep hole and filling it with stones, rubble or builders' aggregate. The pipes should be laid about $2\frac{1}{2}$ ft below the soil surface (75cm) just touching at the joints which are covered with stones or rubble before replacing the excavated soil.

If the roots of the vine are to be restricted within a trough, its floor should slope both from front to back and from end to end, and land drain pipes laid along the lower edge of the trough with an outlet at the

Fig.1. As the bed is enlarged in the first years of growth, good drainage material is placed below the compost mixture.

lowest corner leading to a ditch, surface water drain or a soak-away. A layer of drainage material over the whole of the floor area of the trough will ensure that any excess water finds its way to the drains.

In its first year the young plant will not require a very extensive root-run, and the old practice of making up a narrow border for the first year and adding to the width annually has much to commend it. It ensures that compost full of nutrient and in good physical condition is being added year by year during the formative years of the vine. Concrete building blocks provide a convenient means of retaining the compost during this period.

Preparations for planting include the provision of wires for supporting and training the vines inside the greenhouse. These preferably run at right angles to the line of the rods, spaced at intervals of about 9 inches (22cm) and, ideally, 18 inches (45cm) below the glass. In a small greenhouse it may only be possible to allow 12 or 14 inches from the glass (30-35 cm), but remember that young shoots tend to grow vertically and will soon stub themselves against the glass and become scorched or distorted if they do not have enough space.

Planting
Young vines are usually raised and invariably sold in containers, and therefore planting can be done at any time of the year. November and December are usually convenient months for planting and at that time of year the main stem can be cut back hard, removing at least two thirds of the growth of the previous year. If the plants are not obtained until later in the winter then it is unwise to prune at all as the cut is likely to bleed severely when sap rises in the spring. If planting is done when growth is active leave the main shoot uncut until pruned after leaf-fall.

In a small greenhouse the position of the rod needs careful thought. Planting at the side of the greenhouse and running the stem up to the ridge is not always a practical solution. The alternatives are to plant it centrally at one end of the house and train it along the length of the house under the ridge, or to plant it at one side at the end, near the corner, and run the rod along that side wall. If two or more vines are to be planted next to each other remember that the spread of the lateral growth will require a space of not less than 2 feet (60 cm) on either side of each rod and therefore a distance of at least 4 feet (1.20m) is needed between rods.

The first year
In the first year after planting (and after the initial hard pruning) the main stem is allowed to grow unchecked and encouraged to produce the maximum length of vigorous shoot. If the roots are growing well the main shoot will reach 10 feet or more (3m) and produce lateral shoots over much of its length. These side shoots are cut off during the summer

5

when they have made five or six leaves and any sub-laterals they then produce are cut after making one leaf. Both main stem and laterals are loosely tied into position on the wires as they grow, allowing stems ample room to increase their girth.

At the end of the growing season and as soon as the leaves have fallen the main stem can be cut back hard, removing at least two thirds of the main stem and cutting back the lateral shoots on the remaining section to a plump bud where they join the mainstem.

When grown in a greenhouse most vines are trained to what is known as a rod and spur system, a permanent framework consisting of a main stem with spur growths at intervals of 9 to 12 inches along it (23 to 30cm). The spurs produce new growth each year and with it the fruit, whereas the stem between the spurs is barren. This method of cultivation can be varied by growing two or more rods on one plant or by allowing the rod to branch and extend until one vine fills an entire greenhouse as does the noted vine at Hampton Court. A few skilled growers prefer to grow their vines on a replacement system, training in new rods each year and pruning away the old rods after fruiting but this is not an easy system to manage and is not recommended for the beginner.

Winter pruning of established vines
Ideally the greenhouse should remain quite cold so that the sap flow is inactive. Ventilation can be given freely in all but the severest weather, the main precaution being to give protection against freezing of any hot water heating installation. Prune vines immediately the leaves have fallen—this is usually in late November or December. Pruning cuts made later in the winter stand a real risk of bleeding when the sap rises in the spring. This can be prolonged and may have a debilitating effect on the vine. It is very difficult to stop it and various "cures" have been suggested, but it is better to avoid the trouble rather than to cure it. If pruning has been left rather late then paint the cuts with carpenters' knotting to help prevent bleeding later.

With established rod and spur systems the winter pruning consists of cutting back all growth made in the past year (other than that required for extension or replacement) to within one or two buds of older wood. One bud is enough if it is a strong plump one but often the basal bud is small whereas the second one is strong and plump; with some of the muscat grapes the latter is more likely to produce a good bunch of fruit.

With a vine grown on the replacement system the winter pruning is much the same as that for the single Guyot system of growing vines in the open (see p.27). Two new main stems are grown up each year, one of these is retained for fruiting and the other pruned hard back to two buds to produce the two rods for the following year. The rod which has fruited is cut away completely.

Figs 2 and 3. The glasshouse vine, grown on the rod and spur system of pruning, before (above) and after (below) pruning in midwinter.

The rod and spur system is more easily managed than the replacement system and for that reason is favoured for glasshouse grapes in this country, but if well handled the replacement system will usually give better bunches and larger berries.

Winter maintenance

The practice of scraping away the oldest bark from a rod takes time and is regarded by some as unnecessary, but I believe it is still well worth doing. The old bark fibres on the rods and the loose flakes of bark which cling to the spurs provide good protection for pests such as red spider and mealybug. Much of the fibrous bark can be rubbed or pulled away by hand but some careful scraping with a knife is needed on the spurs, going down to the smooth brown bark but not cutting any green tissue.

The next stage in the winter routine after cleaning the rods is the application of a pesticide. A 4% solution of tar oil winter wash (4 fluid ounces of tar oil in 5 pints of water: 112 cc in $2\frac{1}{2}$ litres) is ideal if the vines are on their own, and if the rather persistent although not harmful smell is unlikely to creep into the home. For the vines in a mixed greenhouse malathion or one of the systemic insecticides can be used; the smell does not persist for long after the application has dried. Although the insecticide can be applied as a spray, the treatment is far more effective if it is painted on with a brush, rubbing it well into crevices and angles in the bark. Wear waterproof gloves and wash off any splashes on the skin immediately. Take care that the buds are not injured and complete the task by early January. This work is more convenient if the rods are

Figs. 4 and 5. Scraping the old fibrous bark off the spur (left) and brushing with tar oil solution (right).

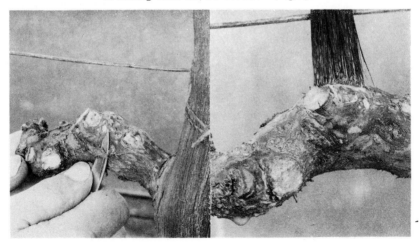

Fig. 6. Renewing the mulch of well-rotted manure in the spring.

untied and lowered from the wires. All of the old string must be removed from the wires as it may harbour pests.

The next job is to renovate the bed. The remains of any old mulch are raked from the bed and the top half or so of the surface soil gently pricked over with a fork. This is then raked or brushed off with a stiff besom. The roots thus exposed are immediately top-dressed with a good loam compost such as John Innes No. 3.

No more needs to be done for the next two or three months, until the vine is started into growth. As the starting time approaches the soil in the bed is given a really thorough soaking with water; a second watering about a week later may be needed if the root area has become very dry during the winter. After watering apply a mulch of well rotted farmyard manure, spent mushroom compost or similar material; this will help to regulate the moisture content of the soil during the growing season.

The spring routine
Vines in a cold house are usually started into growth in March; in a heated house the starting date depends on the needs of the other plants in the greenhouse. For instance, if *Begonia semperflorens,* petunias or other half-hardy annuals are to be raised from seeds, or perhaps aubergines or tomatoes for growing under glass then some heat may be provided for those plants in February.

During the winter the rods are usually left tied loosely to the wires. Before starting the vine into growth, give the rod a single supporting tie about a third of the way up so that the upper part bends over and almost touches the ground. In this way the rising sap is prevented from rushing to the top buds and stimulating them into growth, but is slowed down to induce growth in the side buds all the way up the stem. When the buds on all spurs have started to grow the rods are tied up into their summer position on the wires. Temperatures at this stage may rise rapidly in sunlight, so when the temperature reaches about 19°C (66°F) ventilate the house. If artificial heat is used then a night temperature of 4-7°C (39-45°F) is ample. A gentle start, with the temperatures slowly increased as the vines start to grow should be the aim. The atmosphere should be kept moist by damping down the floor and walls on fine days. Until flowering begins the rods can with advantage be sprayed overhead with clear water early in the mornings but this must be done before the sun becomes hot for there is a risk that the foliage might be burnt by the action of the sun's rays through water droplets.

With the rod and spur system only one shoot is needed on each spur and the standard recommendation is to remove surplus shoots as soon as possible. In practice if they are removed whilst sap pressure is still high there is a risk of bleeding. It is safer to let two shoots develop for a while then pinch the weaker of the two back to two or three leaves. This will give an insurance against a blind spur if a shoot is accidentally broken when tying it in.

Figs 7 and 8. Removing a surplus shoot from a spur (left), and a lateral shoot tied down with a running noose (right).

Tying the young shoots on to the training wires is rather tricky as they easily snap at the junction with the older wood. It can be done safely by catching the shoot and the wire with a running noose, then pulling in the noose a little every other day until the shoot is in position on the wire. It is unwise to tie in while the growth is very young and brittle, and better to wait until a little fibrous tissue has formed. It is a task for early in the morning; if done late in the day the growth may be a little limp and will be easily tied in, but during the night the stems become turgid again and some of the shoots will snap.

Flowering and pollination

By the time 18 to 24 inches of growth has formed (45-60 cm) the flower trusses will be showing and pinching out of the shoot tips can start. Two leaves are allowed to form beyond the flower bunch before the growing tip is removed. If no bunch is formed the shoot is allowed to make 6 or 8 leaves before removing the tip.

Although some cultivars set their fruit very readily it is never wise to leave pollination to chance and with the muscat types it is essential to help the pollination. With free setting cultivars such as 'Black Hamburgh', 'Foster's Seedling' and 'Alicante' all that is needed is to give the rods a brisk shake at mid-day. With the less free setting muscats rather more is needed and the easiest effective method is to stroke the bunches gently with cupped hands so that pollen is collected on the palms of the hands and the fingers and passed on to the receptive stigma. If the

Fig. 9 (left). A stopped shoot showing the formation of laterals.
Fig. 10 (right). A shoot showing a flower truss and later growth.

11

flowers are at the right stage the caps which encased the flowers will be seen falling to the ground as these tasks are performed and the pollen can usually be seen floating slowly down.

Ventilation is very important at this period, with the aim of producing a warm but buoyant (i.e. "moving", not stagnant) atmosphere. This is easily obtained on a sunny day when the ventilators can be opened freely but much more difficult on a dull, cool wet day. Even on a cool day give an inch or so of ventilation. Do not spray overhead on such days.

Thinning the fruit
After fertilisation the tiny grapes will rapidly increase in size, but those imperfectly fertilised will remain smaller or will fall off. If all the bunches set are allowed to mature the quality of the fruit suffers. In addition the vigour of vegetative growth is lost and fruiting is upset; this may affect the vine for several years. The first step therefore in lightening the load is to reduce the number of bunches. This is done as soon as it is possible to see which bunches show promise of being shapely, well set and of good size. Where two bunches are being carried on one spur the less meritorious of the two is removed, the number of bunches then is reduced according to the size of the bunch which the cultivar concerned may normally produce. The aim should be to carry 1lb. of grapes for every foot run of the main stem although this limit can be exceeded slightly if the rod is growing vigorously. With cultivars which carry a moderately sized bunch of 1 to $1\frac{1}{4}$lb (0.5kg) this usually means reducing the number of bunches by one third.

Next the grapes in the remaining bunches should be thinned. This is an operation which requires a little knowledge, and a lot of care, common sense and patience. It is not unduly difficult but it takes time.

Special grape scissors are best for thinning and these are still obtainable but ordinary scissors can also be used, provided that they taper to a point and are sharp particularly at the tip. The second tool which will be needed is a small stick about six inches long forked at one end, which is very easily obtained as it can be fashioned from a hedgerow twig. Grapes should not be touched with fingers until they are eaten otherwise the bloom on the skin will be damaged. This not only spoils the look of the bunch, but removes the extra protection given by the water repellent qualities of the bloom.

A knowledge of the cultivar to be thinned is an advantage as the degree of thinning must suit the characteristics of the bunch. For instance 'Muscat Hamburgh' carries oval grapes on long stalks and is a poor setting type. It is seldom necessary to remove more than a small percentage of the grapes, since if too many are removed a limp, ill-formed bunch is produced. 'Alicante' on the other hand has larger broader grapes on very short stalks and sets very freely, so it needs to be thinned severely. For this cultivar it is necessary to start thinning directly the fruit has set, otherwise the grapes become so crowded that thinning is very difficult.

Fig. 11 (above. A bunch before the first thinning.

Fig. 12 (below). The same bunch after the first thinning.

Fig. 13. A bunch in need of a second thinning.

Fig. 14. The same bunch after the second thinning.

Occasionally it is necessary to trim a bunch into shape before thinning the grapes. Usually this only involves the removal of a straggling arm at the top of the bunch. Any large bunches have their topmost side branches supported by looping them up to the training wires with raffia. The forked stick is used to steady the bunch whilst thinning proceeds. Grapes in the middle of the bunch are cut away first, then any undersized berries as these are probably imperfectly set. Following that, the outer berries are spaced out to allow them room for their growth. Take care not to thin the shoulders of the bunch too much, they should stand out firm and square when the bunch is harvested.

Thinning can seldom be completed in one operation. It is usually necessary to remove a few more grapes three or four weeks after the first thinning and then have a final look over after the pips have formed, when the grapes undergo a second period of swelling.

Watering and feeding
A vine in full leaf will make heavy demands on soil moisture in warm weather and provided that the drainage is good the risk of overwatering is very slight indeed. The intervals at which water is required will vary greatly according to the weather. If the vine's roots are all inside the greenhouse a generous application of water will probably be necessary every 7 to 10 days in hot weather and sufficient should be given to penetrate several feet into the border soil. If the roots are outside they may be supplied by natural rainfall for much of the year but should not be forgotten in prolonged dry spells.

Feeding will be required while growth is active. If growth is poor then a high nitrogen or a general purpose feed may be given early in the summer but if a good quality fruit is to be obtained then high potash feeds are essential. Any of the feeds recommended for use on tomatoes are suitable and should be given at intervals of 2 to 3 weeks until the fruit starts to colour when feeding is stopped.

Ripening
Throughout the summer and autumn a healthy vine will continue to grow vigorously. Any new shoots not needed to fill gaps in the foliage canopy or to add to the length of rod for the following year are cut back after one new leaf is formed; this must be done promptly or the growths will rapidly get out of control. Cut away all tendrils immediately they form.

When the grapes start to change colour the risk of splitting increases. This stage of growth is easily recognised in black or tawny grapes but is not so easily noticed with green ones although there is a slight change of colour towards white or amber. Splitting is encouraged in an atmosphere that is too damp, so do not damp down late in the day and leave a leeside top ventilator open an inch or two at night. Avoid a rapid rise in temperature at any time because the temperature of the grapes rises only slowly, and moisture from the air will condense onto the fruits which may then split. Take care over watering too. If the soil is allowed to get very dry the skins of the grapes will harden and when water is finally given, they will be likely to split. A thin mulch of straw on the bed will help to keep the soil uniformly moist and the air in the greenhouse dry through this period of ripening. If the greenhouse is used for other plants take care to avoid excess drips or splashes especially late in the day. Starting in the early stages of ripening look over the bunches two or three times a week for diseased grapes and those with a split skin, and continue this until the end of the season. Cut out the bad grapes with the vine scissors using the forked stick, and working with care so that the "bloom" is not rubbed from the grapes.

Grapes are not completely ripe even when fully coloured. They need to hang for a further period during which the sugars are formed. This final stage of sweetening is known as the finishing period, and varies with the cultivar and the time of year. 'Black Hamburgh' and 'Foster's Seedling', ripening in summer, need only two or three weeks to finish while 'Muscat of Alexandria' in autumn will take four or five weeks and the late grapes 'Alicante', 'Mrs Pince' and 'Syrian' need to hang for eight to ten weeks before they are at their best.

When harvesting the bunches cut them with a "handle", i.e. cut the branch carrying the bunch about 2 inches (5cm) on either side of the point where it hangs. This handle enables the bunch to be inspected, carried, mounted on a show board or placed on a dish without the fruits being handled and the attractive bloom removed.

Ripe grapes may be kept in good condition on the vine for several weeks by using artificial heat and ventilation to maintain a cool dry atmosphere (about 7°C 45°F). Inspect the bunches daily and remove grapes showing signs of decay immediately. The practice of cutting grapes with a foot of woody stem and storing them with the stems in bottles of water in racks in a dry, dark, closed room at 5-7°C (41-45°F) is not often used now but it can be done with thick skinned, late keeping cultivars such as 'Alicante', 'Gros Colmar', 'Mrs Pince' and 'Syrian'.

2. Vines in pots*

The cultivation of vines in pots has much to commend it. Being portable, the containers can be readily moved within the greenhouse and removed outside after fruiting. Outdoor treatment is important to both ripen the shoots and provide a cold environment during dormancy. If clay pots are used, they should be plunged to lessen possible frost damage but in any case plunging gives stability to any container during windy weather.

*By Ray Waite, RHS Glasshouse Superintendent.

Much of what has already been described regarding the cultivation of vines under glass applies equally to the management of pot-grown grapes and because worthwhile crops can be obtained the method deserves to be more widely adopted, especially for owners of the smaller greenhouse. Where space is limited more than one cultivar can be grown and with care the more usual crops can be cultivated at the same time. Heated or cold glass can be used but the former, of course, gives a longer season of growth and therefore earlier ripening.

Fig. 15. A vine in a pot showing the length of stem before the branches arise.

17

The early fruiting types will be found to be the most satisfactory with 'Black Hamburgh' still possibly the most suitable; but 'Buckland Sweetwater', 'Foster's Seedling' and the Frontignan types all give good results.

Well established rods should be obtained and ideally potted just as the roots become active in the spring. A loam based compost is probably best if for no other reason than to save the plant becoming top heavy. John Innes Potting Compost No. 3 is ideal.

Initially the aim is to build up a strong plant so a young rod in, say a 5-inch pot (13cm) should be moved into a 7-inch (18cm) size, but plants with larger root balls can be moved into a 9-inch (23cm) pot. Before potting and whilst the vine is completely dormant prune the rod back to a bud (eye) at about 4 to 5 feet (1 to 1.5m); however, the height can be determined to suit individual needs.

Once started into growth, the shoots soon lengthen and the top four or

Fig. 16. 'Buckland Sweetwater' showing the new shoots arising from multiple buds.

18

Fig. 17. Branches are secured to the central cane with raffia or garden twine.

five shoots should be left to develop a 'head' being pinched at five to six leaves. The remaining growths should be removed to give a clean stem. Flower clusters are unlikely to appear and in any case should not be allowed to develop at this early stage.

In the second year prune the ripened shoots to one bud and as active growth begins, top dress the container with a rich compost, being careful to leave enough depth for adequate watering. Once again it will be necessary to encourage strong growth and to ensure that it is well ripened by standing the vine out of doors from mid-summer onwards.

During the growing season the application of a balanced fertilizer at regular intervals will be beneficial. Precocious flower clusters should be removed as fruiting is best not encouraged at this stage.

During the third year, as in subsequent years, hard pruning to one good bud should be carried out during the dormant season. A move into a larger container will almost certainly be required although with careful top dressing and feeding a vine can remain in the same final pot for many years.

The first fruit can be expected too, with the growths being pinched at two leaves beyond the bunch and any laterals and sub-laterals pinched at

19

one leaf. The growths will need supporting and this can be done quite simply by means of carefully placed ties attached to a central cane in a maypole fashion. A general fertilizer can be used at this stage but later as the fruits form apply a high potash feed.

In favoured situations it may be possible to finish ripening the fruit outside but care must be taken to prevent damage from birds and wasps.

3. Vines for greenhouse cultivation

Of the wide range of grapes which were grown under glass at the start of the century only a few are now in cultivation and even fewer are available from commercial sources.

Disregarding fruit colour greenhouse grapes fall into three groups;
SWEETWATER (S). These are early grapes, quick to mature and ripen. They are ideally suited for an unheated greenhouse. They are very sweet and juicy but without the muscat flavour. They have very thin skins when at their best but do not hang on the vine in good condition for long.
MUSCATS (M) are the finest grapes for flavour, but they need heat. They are the second group to mature and they hang well in good condition if a little warmth is provided. The fruit is firm and luscious and if allowed to hang until the skin starts to wrinkle the berries often take on the flavour of raisins. They are unfortunately difficult to get to set well unless they have warmth and some manual assistance with pollination.
VINOUS (V). These are the really late grapes and in the past were grown to provide fruit well into the new year. They are usually strong growing and crop well but need to hang for a long time in a warm greenhouse to develop their best flavour. They are not a worthwhile proposition unless heat can be provided for them in the early winter months.

Alicante (V). A black (late) grape. Vigorous grower. Fruit sets freely and needs early and severe thinning. It is inclined to form an unshapely bunch but when well thinned it can produce a handsome and imposing bunch for show with its large, almost round, jet-black berries covered in heavy blue/grey bloom (9 medium-size bunches/12 feet of rod).*
Black Hamburgh (S) has the best flavour of this group and is justifiably the grape best known and most widely grown under glass in this country. Of good constitution, it sets fruit freely and can be ripened well in an unheated greenhouse. If allowed to hang too long after ripening the skin becomes very thin and easily broken and the fruit deteriorates. (12 medium-size bunches/12 feet of rod).
Buckland Sweetwater (S). A round white grape carried in short broad bunches. It sets freely and ripens early. It has a pleasant flavour when in
*These figures are given as a guide to a reasonable number of bunches per healthy vine.

good condition but the skin thickens and the fruit deteriorates if it is allowed to hang too long on the vine. It is not a very vigorous cultivar and needs to be fed well for good results. (12 bunches/12 feet of rod).

Canon Hall Muscat (M) is an almost round white grape which becomes pale amber on ripening. Of excellent flavour when well grown. Berries very large. Widely grown on Guernsey but is a difficult grape to grow well unless heat is provided at flowering time and for ripening the fruit.

Frontignan (M). Both the black and the white Frontignan grapes may be considered together. They are early maturing with small grapes of good quality. Well suited to growing in pots under glass. (14 bunches/12 feet).

Foster's Seedling (S). The best of the white sweetwater grapes. It sets freely, the bunches are of medium size and shapely, the grapes oval, juicy and of a pleasant flavour, ripening early. They should be eaten fairly soon after ripening or they will lose flavour. It has a good constitution and grows well in an unheated greenhouse. (12 bunches/12 feet).

Gros Colmar (V). A strong growing, round, black grape, with very large fruits and handsome bunches. The skin is thick and the flavour poor until the fruit has had a long period of ripening in a warm greenhouse through the early winter. (10 bunches/12 feet).

Lady Downe's Seedling (V) One of the better flavoured vinous grapes with round black berries carried in long tapering bunches. It is of good constitution but requires warmth at flowering time to ensure a good set of berries and in the early winter to ripen its fruit. (10 bunches/12 feet).

Lady Hutt (S) is a round white grape ripening several weeks later than others in that group. It is a robust grower, sets freely and produces large bunches of thin-skinned juicy berries. (5 bunches/12 feet).

Madresfield Court (M) is an early ripening oval, black grape of high quality. Its berries are large and covered with dense blue/grey bloom, the flesh firm but juicy and of good flavour, but the skin is tough. The berries are liable to split on ripening and for this reason some growers used to leave top shoots to run on without stopping at ripening to reduce sap pressure. (10 bunches/12 feet).

Mrs Pearson (M) is a round white grape which ripens late. It grows strongly, sets freely, bears fruit of excellent flavour but with thick skins and will hang in good condition after ripening. It does however need warmth throughout the ripening and holding period. (10 bunches/12 feet).

Mrs Pince (M) is a strong growing, oval, black grape which produces late grapes of excellent quality but requires warmth and hand pollination at flowering to obtain a good set of fruits. It requires warmth throughout the early winter when it is ripening. (10 bunches/12 feet).

Muscat of Alexandria (M). When well grown there is no better flavoured grape. It has a good constitution but needs warmth and hand pollination if it is to set a good crop of oval white grapes. Warmth is also needed to ripen the fruit although if heat is used in the greenhouse in spring to start the vine into growth early the grapes should ripen in the September sunshine. (10 bunches/12 feet).

Muscat Hamburgh (M). An oval, black grape of excellent quality which ripens before most of the other muscats. It is sometimes recommended for growing in an unheated house but it is difficult to grow well. It needs warmth and hand pollination at flowering time (cross pollination, using pollen from a different cultivar is helpful). Although it is fairly vigorous in growth it has a strong tendency to shank (see p.44). (9 bunches/12 feet).

Syrian (V). A late, oval, white grape of great vigour. It will rapidly get out of control unless regularly pruned in summer. It carries impressively large bunches but the flavour is poor unless they are allowed to hang in a warm house until Christmas. (5 bunches/12 feet).

Trebbiano (V). An oval, white late grape similar in many respects to 'Syrian'. It is notable for the size of the bunches, one of which is on record as weighing 26lb 4oz. (5 bunches/12 feet).

4. Propagation

Vine cuttings will root very readily. Soft, green cuttings taken in summer need some heat for rooting but hardwood cuttings taken in winter can if necessary be rooted outside.

Material for hardwood cuttings is selected when the vines are pruned in December. It can be temporarily stored in the open garden until the cuttings are made, by digging a small trench, putting in the cuttings, and covering the bases. This will keep the base moist until the time for making cuttings. If they are to be rooted in the open, cut the prunings to about 8 inches long (20cm), with three buds. Make a cut above the top bud and another just below the lower bud before inserting the cutting to a depth of about 6 inches (15cm) in sandy well-drained soil. Rooting is also possible in containers in a cold frame; a cutting of two buds will be much more convenient to insert in a pot. If cuttings of this type are inserted singly in $3\frac{1}{2}$-inch pots in a compost consisting of two parts sand, one part loam and one part peat in January they should be well rooted by early June. They may then be potted on into 5-inch pots in John Innes No. 2 potting compost. Those cuttings rooted in the open garden should remain undisturbed until the following autumn.

With more sophisticated apparatus such as a heated propagating case, single bud cuttings are usually inserted in January singly in $2\frac{1}{2}$-inch pots in a compost of equal parts of peat and sand with bottom heat of 18°C (64°F). These are made with a cut just above the bud and another about 2 inches below (5cm). They are pressed vertically into the surface of the soil mixture (sand, loam and peat as above) with the bud just clear of the surface. Other methods involving a horizontally inserted single bud cutting may be found in old literature but these are no more effective.

Greenwood cuttings may be made in July or August, using shoots of the current year. Lengths of stem about 4 inches (10cm) are cut just below a bud, to include either the growing tip or at least two buds. These are inserted in a mixture of equal parts of peat and sand in a pot, in a propagating case they will root readily with a bottom heat of 18°C (64°F) in six or eight weeks. As with the single bud cuttings these are best propagated in 2½-inch pots so that undue root disturbance is avoided when potting is required. The first move should be into 3½-inch pots and John Innes No. 1 potting compost and then when the plants are sufficiently robust they should be potted on again into 5-inch pots and John Innes No. 2 potting compost. In their first year the young vines, although perfectly hardy, will make better growth if kept in a cool greenhouse.

Vines can be grafted and some commercial growers of wine grapes in this country take the precautions of grafting their vines onto rootstocks which are resistant to attack by a root pest, *Phylloxera vastatrix,* which has over the years been a major worry to owners of continental vineyards (see p.41). Fortunately this is not a pest which the amateur grower of vines is likely to meet, and the need for grafting is therefore unlikely to arise.

5. Vines in the open

The vine is a sun loving plant and happiest outside on a warm wall; nevertheless, grapes can be grown out in the open, at least in the south, and further north where there is a favourable microclimate, provided the right cultivars are chosen. Thanks originally to the work of a few pioneer viticulturists, principally Mr Barrington Brock in the 1950s, a number of grapes have proved reasonably successful outside and more have been introduced since. However, even with the correct choice of cultivar, grapes will only fruit successfully and the berries acquire sugar content and flavour for good wine in warm, dry summers, and of course without frost at flowering time. They will not do well in areas of high summer rainfall, strong winds or where the climate is cool during the growing season.

In general, outdoor grapes can be planted south of a line from the Wash in the east to south Wales in the west. Further north than this, it is best to grow the vine on a wall or provide some kind of protection and even in the south the use of glass or plastic to protect against frost and as a means to increase the temperature is very beneficial.

In essence, the United Kingdom is a marginal area, and whilst there will be vintage years, there will be others when the resultant wine will be regarded even by the best of friends as "vin ordinaire".

Site

With vines grown in the open the choice of site is most important. It must be sheltered and yet in full sun and at an elevation of not more than 300 feet. The ideal site is a south or south westerly slope, though this is by no means essential. Avoid planting in a frost pocket as frost in the late spring can damage the blossom and young growth, possibly wiping out the potential crop for that summer. In situations where the gardener has no alternative, he should be prepared to protect the vines by various methods, for example by covering them with hessian, when frost is expected.

Grapes on walls and fences are in the best position because of the reflected warmth from the structure. It must be sunny and sheltered, however, and ideally one with a southerly aspect, though a west facing wall or fence is acceptable.

Soil preparation and planting

The vine is tolerant of a wide range of soils provided they are of reasonable depth, say, not less than 12 inches (30cm), and well drained. Because the grape is deep rooted, this latter point is vital. Heavy clay soils where there are drainage difficulties should be avoided. Very acid soils require to be limed to bring the pH up to between 6.5 and 7.0. With chalky soils the plants may suffer from chlorosis, though it is possible to obtain vines on rootstocks more suited to alkaline conditions (see page 37).

If the land tends to become waterlogged, some kind of drainage system must be installed as the first stage of soil preparation. The type depends upon the scale of planting. In a small area, where only one or two vines are planted, a simple soak-away constructed of broken bricks, clinker and rubble would suffice, but for larger areas, say for a row of vines or more, a length of tile or plastic drains or even a herring bone system of drains may be necessary.

The planting site should be prepared well beforehand by double digging to break up any hard layers. Ensure the area is free of weeds, and add lime if necessary. Too rich a soil is undesirable and no bulky organic manure is required unless the ground is poor. Even then only a light dressing of well rotted manure or compost at the bottom of each trench should be applied. In the final preparations rake in John Innes base fertilizer at the rate of 3 oz per square yard (100 g/m^2).

Plant at any time from October to March. Weak vines, of less than pencil thickness, are best over-wintered under the protection of a cold frame and planted out when the danger of frost is over. Most plants supplied by nurserymen will be on their own roots, although a number of plants are being imported from the continent which are grafted. The latter are resistant to the vine louse, *Phylloxera vastatrix,* though

Fig. 18. A pot grown vine, with a good root system, before planting.

Fig. 19 (below). The vine in the planting hole, with the roots well spread out.

fortunately this is not a problem in this country. Some rootstocks are more suited to alkaline conditions than others (see page 37).

Firm planting is essential and the roots of the young vines (often pot grown) must be carefully spread out to encourage quick establishment. Subsequently mulch them with a little rotted manure or compost so that the lower buds are covered for the winter. With grafted plants the union should certainly be covered in winter. In the spring the mulch should be gently pulled away from the stem. The graft union must be above soil level to prevent scion rooting.

Growing on walls, fences and pergolas

The vine is a climbing plant amenable to many forms of training – the cordon, espalier and fan for example. Whatever the method used, it should be grown in such a way that a permanent framework of branches is maintained.

On walls and solid fences, it is usually grown as a vertical cordon (rod) in single or multiple form with each rod spaced 4 feet (1.2m) apart to allow room for the laterals carrying fruit. On a low fence or under a window the vine could be grown as an espalier with each horizontal arm spaced about 18 inches (45cm) above or below its neighbour. Plant about 9 inches (22cm) away from the wall or fence.

Support. A wall trained grape requires a support system of wires generally taken horizontally and secured to the wall with lead wall eyes. Galvanised fencing wire, gauge 14, spaced 10 to 12 inches can be used (25-30cm) apart.

Training. The strongest shoot is selected to form the rod and after leaf fall is pruned back to a bud where it has become well hardened and woody. Any side shoots are cut back to leave two buds nearest the base. This leading shoot is extended each summer until the desired length is reached and is shortened as just described each winter. If several rods are required from the same vine the first move must be to establish two horizontal shoots. From these the desired number of vertical rods are then developed in subsequent seasons.

Pruning. Pruning, de-shooting and pinching must be done regularly and the method is the same as that described under glass (see pp. 5-6) except that the timing may obviously be different. Over-cropping must be avoided; a young vine in particular will frequently remain barren for a number of years after it has been allowed to carry too many bunches. Two or three bunches only should be allowed on a 3-year-old vine, perhaps four or five in the following year and so on, provided growth is sufficiently vigorous to sustain the crop.

Watering. Adequate soil moisture is vital at all times and since soil close to walls can often be dry, it is important to water regularly as required and before drought conditions have been reached.

Feeding. See under vines in the open (p. 27).

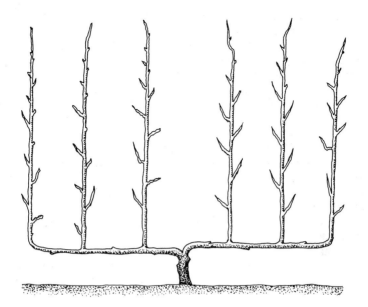

Fig. 20. Diagram of training a vine against a wall, showing how the fruiting arms are trained.

Growing vines in the open

Just as with the grape on a wall there are many methods by which a vine can be trained. It could, for example, be grown in a sunny corner as a vertical cordon trained up a stout pole or even as a kind of half standard reminiscent of a weeping standard rose. The grape in these instances would be spur pruned in the winter and the laterals pinched back in the summer to keep the plant in shape. For vineyards large and small, however, the most widely used method is the Guyot system in single or double form. The single Guyot has one fruit carrying arm, whereas the more popular double Guyot has two. In either form the fruit-carrying arms are trained fairly close to the ground thus taking full advantage of the reflected and radiated warmth from the soil which is so important in the ripening of the berries in our northerly climate.

Basically the "Guyot" is a replacement system of pruning whereby the wood which has fruited in the previous summer is cut out each winter and new wood tied in. It should be noted that some vines may grow rather too weakly to produce sufficiently strong replacement shoots to withstand winter frosts especially in the early years, and these are best grown initially in the espalier form with the laterals pruned back to two buds each winter. Experience will indicate which is the most suitable for your conditions.

Fig. 21. (opposite top left). Pruning at the end of the first year. The young vine is cut to a bud just below the bottom wire.

Fig. 22. (opposite top right). Young vine at the end of the second year; the three shoots have been trained up the cane.

Fig. 23. (opposite below). Two shoots are tied down, one in each direction, and are cut back to 2 to $2\frac{1}{2}$ feet (60 – 75cm). The central shoot has been cut back to 3 or 4 buds.

Fig. 24. (Above). A mature vine at the end of the season. Note the two fruiting arms, one to the left and one to the right, and the three replacement shoots in the middle.

Support. The Guyot system calls for a stout fence of posts and wires. The posts should be spaced at 8 to 10 feet apart (2.5-3m) depending upon the spacing of the plants within the row. The posts are 6½ feet (2m) of 2¾-3 in. diameter (7.5cm) for the end posts and 6½ feet (2m) of 2 in. diameter (5cm) for intermediates, driven 2 feet (60cm) into the ground. Obviously the wood must be preserved against rot and the fence strutted at each end. The wire should consist of 12 (2.5mm) and 14 gauge (2mm) galvanised wire or army surplus insulated telephone wire. The two lowest wires are single and the upper wires are double. Secure the wires to the end posts with straining bolts and the intermediates with staples. The two lower wires (12 gauge/2.5mm) are set at 15 inches and 21 inches from the ground (37cm and 53cm) and the upper (14 gauge/2.00mm) at 3, 4 and 5 feet (90cm, 1.2 and 1.5m). See Fig.24. Preferably the rows should run north to south. If one side of each of the three sets of double wires can be taken down at the time of winter pruning, the task is much easier. To do this fix a short length of chain to the ends of the wires and instead of wire staples on the intermediates use small cup hooks. The chain is pulled round the end post so that the projecting end of the straining bolt is caught in one of its links. Please see photograph.

Spacing, planting and initial pruning. Space the vines at 4 feet (1.2m) in the row: 5 feet (1.5m) may be better in good soils. The spacing between the rows is 5 to 6 feet (1.5m). If a grass sward is preferred, then space the rows 6 feet apart (1.8m) with a clean grass-free band of 18 inches wide (45cm) maintained down the row.

The young vines should be planted to a stout cane or to a supporting fence post where this occurs. Plant to the same depth as the vine was in the nursery, being careful not to bury the graft union under the soil's surface where grafted plants are used.

Normally, the vines will break into growth some time in May. In the first year, only one shoot should be allowed to grow and be trained up the cane, all others being pinched out. In November cut the vine down to just below the bottom wire. In the second summer train in three shoots, tied vertically, pinching back the remainder to one leaf. At the end of the second summer after leaf fall the Double Guyot System begins (see Figs. 20 and 24). One shoot is tied down to the left and one to the right onto the lowest wire. The third shoot is cut to three buds and this will provide the three replacement shoots for the next year. The arms should not overlap with their neighbours, but should be cut to a bud just short of the next vine. Immature wood at the end of each arm should always be removed.

A weak plant with growth of less than pencil thickness when planted is best left unpruned for a year, and then trained and pruned as above.

Water the young plants in the event of dry weather during the growing season and give them an occasional liquid feed.

Fig. 25. Chain fixed to the end of the wire, so that the wire is easily removed for winter pruning.

Cropping. In the first year of fruiting, two or three bunches only should be allowed on a 3-year-old vine, perhaps four or five in the next year, and full cropping thereafter, provided that growth is healthy and vigorous enough to sustain the crop.

Feeding and watering. In February apply Growmore fertilizer at 2 oz per sq. yd. ($66g/m^2$) plus sulphate of potash at $\frac{1}{2}$ oz per sq. yd. ($15g/m^2$) along each side of the row to a width of 1 foot (30cm) on either side. In the spring mulch the vines with a generous dressing of mushroom compost or well rotted garden compost to a depth of about 2 to 3 inches (7cm). Vines are prone to a magnesium deficiency, sometimes evidenced by yellowing of the leaves in summer, but is not to be confused with chlorosis due to alkaline conditions. If magnesium deficiency symptoms occur, apply a foliar spray of $\frac{1}{2}$ lb. magnesium sulphate (coarse Epsom salts) in $2\frac{1}{2}$ gallons of water (220g/11litres) plus a few drops of mild liquid detergent and repeat the spray 14 days later. Thereafter apply the magnesium sulphate as a top dressing in the late spring at 2 oz per sq. yd. ($66g/m^2$).

With dessert grapes give the plants an occasional liquid feed in the growing season, say once weekly, but not after the berries start to ripen.

Well established vines are usually able to cope with dry weather except on very shallow soils, nevertheless it is advisable to water them in drought conditions.

Fig. 26. (opposite). Diagram of pruning a mature vine.

Pruning the established vine

Top. November. Prune as soon as possible after leaf fall, but no later than the end of January. However, early winter pruning stimulates earlier bud burst (by about 7 days) than vines pruned in the spring. Possibly where vines are planted in areas prone to spring frosts, there may be an advantage in pruning in March or April in the hope that they may escape frost damage, but it must be noted that late pruned vines can "bleed" badly from the pruning cuts. Nevertheless, provided the vines are healthy, the bleeding does not appear to weaken the plants and the flow stops once the plant has developed some leaves. Note, there are, or should be, three strong replacement shoots trained up the cane or post. If there aren't, utilise three strong laterals, nearest to the centre. The two arms which bore fruit last summer are cut back to the replacement shoots. One shoot is then tied down to the left and another to the right arching over the lower wires and the third is cut to 3 or 4 buds. These buds will provide the replacement shoots for next year.

Centre. January. Winter pruning completed. Replacement shoots tied on lower wire and immature wood cut off, leaving 2 to $2\frac{1}{2}$ feet each side (60-75cm). Third shoot cut to 3 or 4 buds.

Below. July, August, September. The fruit carrying laterals are trained through the double wires. Prune them to 2 or 3 leaves above the top wires as, and when, necessary, using secateurs or shears. Remove any sub-laterals. The replacement shoots (3 for a Double Guyot, 2 for a Single Guyot) are trained up the cane or post and stopped at about 5 feet (1.5m). Sub-laterals are pinched to one leaf, and as a counsel of perfection, any blossom on the replacement shoots should be removed, though this is not stricly necessary if the growth is strong. Remove any surplus shoots or suckers coming off the main trunk below the two arms. Starting in early September, gradually remove a *small* proportion of the lower leaves, just sufficient to expose the bunches to more sunlight and improve air circulation. Be careful not to expose the bunches too suddenly to the sun as this may lead to sun scorch. This reduction of foliage will help in the ripening of the berries and the control of botrytis.

Spray programme. Details of the diseases which may attack outdoor vines are given on pp. 35-38. But there are two groups of sprays that should be applied as a routine, as follows:

Mid-June: systemic fungicide, wettable sulphur or sulphur dust for powdery mildew control. Repeat 4 times at fortnightly intervals. (N.B. the minimum interval between spraying and harvesting is 7 days).

Just before the flowers open: systemic fungicide for botrytis control. Repeat every 14 days until 3 weeks before harvest.

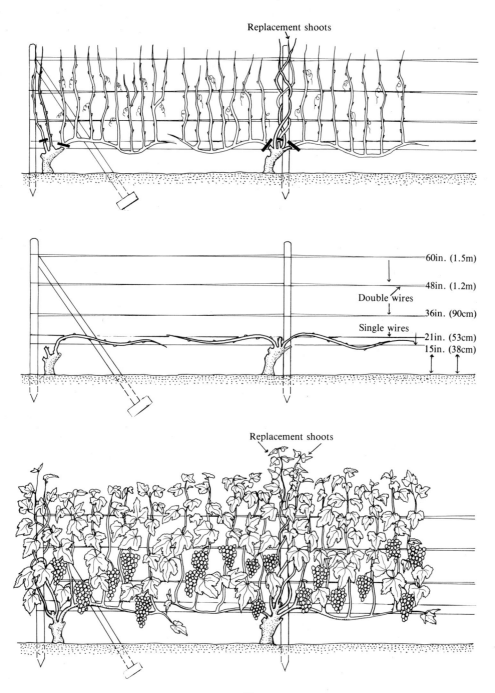

Replacement shoots

60in. (1.5m)

48in. (1.2m)

Double wires

36in. (90cm)

Single wires

21in. (53cm)

15in. (38cm)

Replacement shoots

33

Fig. 27. Above far left, the left hand fruiting arm is cut away. Top left, the right hand fruiting arm is pruned out. Below, the three replacement shoots are left: one arm is tied to the wire at the left, and one to the right. Finally, the third shoot is cut back to 3 buds, each of which will produce a replacement shoot next summer.

Weed control in the open

It is important to control weeds in the first year of planting when the vine is trying to become established as well as in subsequent years when the plant is bearing a crop. Weeds compete for water and nutrients and also are liable to create humid conditions around the bunches making fruits more prone to grey mould. A fairly simple herbicide programme can be adopted using the weed killers simazine and paraquat. Simazine is applied to the soil and is taken up by the germinating weed seeds before emergence. It will not kill weed seedlings that have already emerged nor established weeds. It is used to keep clean land free from weeds. This herbicide creates a seal or barrier to germinating seeds over the surface and the best results are obtained by applying it when the soil is moist, firm and has a fine tilth. It is important to observe the manufacturer's rate of application which should be varied according to whether the soil is light, medium or heavy. Simazine is persistent and the effect should last for about six or seven months. Over-dosing can render the soil sterile and damage the plants. Simazine is applied as an over-all spray; the established fruit plants, if wetted, will not be harmed provided the recommended dosage is used.

Paraquat will kill any green tissue, green bark, green buds or leaves on contact. It has a burning or scorching action and should be directed onto the weeds, but must be kept clear of the vines. Paraquat will kill annual weeds, and perennial weeds that have no underground food reserves.

Apply the simazine to clean, moist soil in February or March and this should last until the second application after cropping in October. Should any weeds appear in the row during the growing season, these can be killed by a carefully directed application of paraquat avoiding the foliage of the vines.

In no circumstances use the hormone based weed killers on or near vines as these are liable to cause severe distortion. (See p. 44.)

6. Cultivars for growing outside

In general, white cultivars, which ripen early October to mid October in the south, are to be preferred for vines in the open. The early ones are very liable to attack by wasps and unless the grower is prepared to protect the bunches, a substantial loss of crop will occur. Nevertheless, further north the early cultivars should be chosen rather than the late which might not ripen. The black grape, other than the hybrids with American species in their parentage, e.g. *Vitis labrusca,* does not do well except in very hot summers with protection, or on a warm, south facing wall. The hybrid is reputed to make a poor quality wine. For these reasons in most commercial vineyards in Britain white grapes predominate.

Because of the popularity of viticulture at the present time, increasing numbers of new cultivars are being imported from the Continent. It is too soon to comment as to their suitability, though no doubt in time some of them at least will prove to be acceptable. Those commonly grown under glass should not be planted in the open. Of the older cultivars, those listed below have proved to be reasonably satisfactory. The season of ripening refers to the south of England.

WHITE

Siegerrebe (very early). A golden brown berry of good flavour with a trace of muscat and high sugar content. Prone to wasps. Dessert and wine. Medium vigour. Late August – early September.

Precoce de Malingre (early). A large berried non-muscat dessert/wine grape of good flavour. Poor to moderate vigour. Light cropper. Late September.

Madeleine Angevine 7972 (early). A heavy cropper. Vigorous. Prone to mildew. Relatively hardy. Suitable for colder areas. White wine. Quality only fair. Late September – early October.

Muller Thurgau (Riesling Sylvaner) (mid season). The most widely planted. It has a delicate flavour and gives an excellent wine, passable as dessert. Needs good weather during pollination. Mid October. Highly recommended.

Seyval (Seyve Villard 5.276) (mid-season). A hybrid, resistant to powdery and downy mildew. A heavy cropper and easy to grow. Blends well with Muller Thurgau. Recommended. Mid to end October.

Chasselas (late). Of which there are a number of clones, e.g. Chasselas d'Or, Chasselas 1921, Chasselas Rose Royale and Royal Muscadine. All yield good quality berries excellent for dessert and wine: however, this cultivar is too late in the open and is better on walls. Late October.

BLACK

Noir Hatif de Marseilles (early). Small black fruits with slight muscat flavour. Dessert. Rather weak grower and requires good soil conditions.

Needs protection or a warm wall. Late September.

Cascade (Seibel 13.053) (midseason). Resistant to mildew. Low in sugar and high in acid. A fair quality wine. Small bunches of deep purple berries with red juice. Very vigorous, excellent as a wall cover plant. Early October.

Brant (late). A hybrid of Canadian origin often grown for its autumn colour, bears heavy crops of small, sweet black grapes, liked by children. Some resistance to mildew. Vigorous, useful wall cover. Mid October.

Strawberry Grape (late). There are a number of clones with black, pink and lime-green berries. Bears small bunches of rather large grapes, flavour fair only and faintly reminiscent of strawberries. Late October. Better grown against a warm wall.

Pinot Noir. A heavy cropper of good quality large black berries, but will not ripen fully outside without protection. Late October. Wine, and acceptable as dessert.

PROMISING CULTIVARS

Scheurebe. A white wine grape. Mid-season, similar to Muller Thurgau, but a heavier cropper. Mid October.

Reichensteiner. A white grape, high in sugar, but makes a neutral wine. Crops heavily. Some resistance to botrytis. Early October.

Huxelrebe. A white grape, producing a good quality muscat flavoured wine slightly earlier than Muller Thurgau. Susceptible to mildew. A heavy cropper. Early October.

Rootstocks

Most vines supplied by nurserymen are on their own roots and these are satisfactory provided *Phylloxera* does not become a problem in this country. Imported vines are grafted onto rootstocks which are resistant to this pest and some have the added advantages of influencing vigour and being more suited to certain soil conditions as follows:—

		Suitability for soil types			
Shallow poor, stony, dry	Deep fertile without chalk	Deep fertile with chalk	Heavy clay with chalk	Heavy clay	Chalk
5BB 125AA	5C SO4 125AA	5C SO4 5BB 125AA	SO4	125AA 5BB SO4	SO4

7. Pests*

Grapes grown out of doors are generally much less liable to be attacked by pests troublesome in greenhouses such as mealybugs, scale insects, red spider mite and whitefly. However, an outdoor vine growing in a warm sheltered position, such as against a south facing wall, may also have these problems. When controlling pests there is a danger that the bloom on glasshouse grapes will be marred if sprays are applied after the fruits have begun to swell. As far as possible, pests should be controlled before this stage is reached, or formulations less likely to affect the bloom, such as smokes or aerosols, should be used. Insecticides should not be used within 10 days of picking the fruit.

The first five pests listed below all have a wide range of host plants. If the vine is being grown in a greenhouse with other plants, these should also be checked for the presence of pests and treated accordingly.

Scale insects. Scale insects feed by sucking sap from the vine and the type most commonly found is called brown scale. The mature insects are covered by hard, shiny brown, convex shells about $\frac{1}{4}$ inch (6mm) long and they are attached to the vine stems. Apart from the recently hatched nymphs, scale insects do not move once they have found a suitable feeding place.

A less common but more spectacular type of scale insect is the woolly vine scale. The mature females of this scale have dark brown, wrinkled shells about $\frac{3}{16}$ inch (4mm) in diameter, which are perched on the edge of a mass of white waxy threads which contains the eggs.

Scale insects can be controlled by thoroughly brushing the vine rods with a tar oil wash during December. Tar oil will damage any plants that are in leaf, so care must be taken if other plants are growing nearby. Before treatment, the vine rods should be scraped to remove loose bark and as many scales as possible. The scrapings should be collected and burnt. If necessary, the vine can also be sprayed with malathion in late June and mid July as the young nymphs begin to hatch.

Mealybug. This is a common pest of glasshouse grapes. Mealybugs are soft bodied, pinkish grey insects up to $\frac{1}{8}$ inch (3mm) long, and they suck sap from the leaves and stems. They tend to cluster in the leaf axils and they secrete white woolly fibres around themselves. They excrete a sugary substance called honeydew that makes the vine sticky and encourages the growth of a black sooty mould on the surface of the foliage and fruits.

The winter tar oil treatment described above under scale insects also deals with mealybugs. If they persist during the growing season they can be controlled by thorough spraying with malathion at 14-day intervals during the spring and early summer.

Glasshouse red spider mite. Red spider mites are tiny, eight-legged, sap-

*By Andrew Halstead, RHS Entomologist.

feeding animals that occur in large numbers on the underside of the leaves. They overwinter as adult mites and they begin feeding on the new foliage during April or May. The first sign of an attack is a fine yellowish green speckling that can be seen on the upper leaf surface; examination of the underside of the leaf with a hand lens should reveal the mites. As the infestation increases, leaves begin to dry up and drop off, and the vine may become covered in a fine silken webbing which is produced by the mites. Despite their common name, the mites are not really red and they range in colour from nearly black to yellowish green or orange.

Early treatment is required to prevent a damaging infestation from developing. As soon as mite damage is seen, the vine should be sprayed with malathion with further applications at 7- to 14-day intervals as necessary. As an alternative to using pesticides, red spider mite can be controlled by introducing a predatory mite called *Phytoseiulus persimilis*, although this cannot be used if insecticides are being used to control other pests. Supplies can be obtained from: Natural Pest Control (Amateur), Watermead, Yapton Road, Barnham, Bognor Regis, West Sussex PO22 0BQ; Bunting and Sons, The Nurseries, Great Horksley, Colchester, Essex.

Glasshouse whitefly. Adult whiteflies are tiny moth-like insects with white wings which live on the underside of the leaves. The nymphal stages are flat, whitish green scales, and both the adults and nymphs feed by sucking sap. Like mealybugs, whitefly can create problems with honeydew and sooty mould. The eggs and nymphal stages are relatively immune to insecticides, so frequent sprays are necessary to kill the adults as they develop.

Sprays containing permethrin or related compounds, such as resmethrin or pyrethrum, are effective. As an alternative to insecticides, a parasitic wasp called *Encarsia formosa* can be introduced during the summer. This is available from the same sources as *Phytoseiulus* (see above).

Vine weevil. The adult weevils feed at night and eat irregular shaped notches from the leaf margins of many plants, including grape vine. The beetles are mainly black with small brown patches on the wing cases. The slow moving beetles are about $\frac{3}{8}$ inch (9mm) long and they have elbowed antennae. Their larvae are fat, creamy white, legless grubs with brown heads. They live in the soil and feed on roots. Well established vines are unlikely to suffer serious damage, but pot-grown or young vines may be killed by the grubs. If damage caused by the grubs or adults is seen, they can be controlled by drenching the soil with a spray strength mixture of HCH (BHC).

Vine blister mite (Erinose). This is a microscopic mite that can occur on both glasshouse and outdoor grapes. It overwinters inside the buds and starts feeding on the leaves in the spring. As a result of this feeding, the

Fig. 28 (left). Fruit protected from wasps by an old nylon stocking.
Fig. 29 (right). Net supported over vines to protect fruit from bird damage.

upper surface of the leaves develops raised patches and the underside of these blisters is covered by fine white hairs. These hairs may be confused with mildew disease but the blistering effect is diagnostic for the mites. The symptoms first appear in May or June, and as the summer progresses the hairs darken and become reddish brown. The mites live among the hairs and feed on the leaf surface but, apart from some disfigurement to the leaves, they seem to cause no real harm. Infestations can usually be dealt with by picking off the affected leaves.

Wasps. In some years wasps are very numerous and they will damage large numbers of grapes, especially of the early ripening varieties. An effort should be made to find and destroy as many wasp nests as possible in the locality. It is easier to follow the wasps' flight paths as the sun is setting and likely places to look for nests are ditches, hedge bottoms, and under the eaves of buildings. Once located, the nests can be destroyed by placing a wasp powder such as carbaryl in the entrance hole. Individual bunches of grapes can be protected from wasps by enclosing them in bags made from muslin or old nylon stockings. Wasps can also be kept out of greenhouses by screening the ventilators with nylon netting.

Birds. Birds are the most damaging pests of outdoor grapes and they may eat the entire crop unless the vine is covered with bird-proof netting. This will need to be in place from the beginning of September to the middle of October depending on the cultivars grown. Netting with a mesh of $\frac{3}{4}$-inch or an inch (19-25mm) must be used. If the vine is too large to be com-

Fig. 30. Trim summer shoots to 6 inches (15cm) above the top wire.

pletely netted, individual bunches can be enclosed in bags made from muslin or nylon stockings.

Vine phylloxera. This serious pest of vines does not occur in Britain at the present time. It is an aphid-like insect with a complex life cycle, having different forms that cause galls on the roots and the leaves. Infested plants are killed or severely stunted, although the effects of this pest are less devastating now that phylloxera-resistant rootstocks are available. Suspected outbreaks of this pest should be reported to the local office of the Ministry of Agriculture.

8. Diseases and disorders*

Diseases

Grey mould is the most troublesome disease on outdoor vines, but it can also be a nuisance on indoor grapes in poorly ventilated greenhouses where humidity is high.

Affected grapes rot and become covered with a dense brownish grey furry mass of fungal growth. The fungus either attacks the berries through wounds or it may invade the floral parts so that some of the fruits are already diseased as they develop. By whichever method infection occurs, once the disease is established it can spread rapidly by contact and also by means of air-borne spores which are produced in vast

*By Audrey V. Brooks, RHS Plant Pathologist.

numbers. In wet weather and in very humid greenhouses crop loss can be considerable. Under glass the trouble can be prevented to a certain extent by adequate ventilation to reduce the humidity and by the prompt removal of unhealthy berries and leaves. Once the disease has occurred fumigate the greenhouse with tecnazene smokes.

It is difficult to control the disease on outdoor grapes so in wet seasons try to improve the aeration around the bunches by thinning out some of the berries and judicious removal of some of the shoots. Sprays of benomyl, carbendazim or thiophanate-methyl will control grey mould for a season or two, but regular use of these fungicides may lead to the development of strains of the fungus which are resistant to them so that they will become ineffective. For those growing grapes on a commercial scale, fungicides are available to control this disease, and advice should be sought on this subject.

Powdery mildew is most troublesome on indoor vines particularly in a cold greenhouse especially if the soil is dry and the atmosphere is humid or stagnant. Powdery mildew is also common on outdoor grapes, particularly on those growing in very dry positions such as against walls. A white powdery coating of fungus spores develops on young shoots and leaves but occasionally the fungus develops only sparsely and then the most obvious symptom is a grey or purplish discoloration of the diseased areas. The disease can also attack the flowers and fruits causing them to

Fig. 31. Powdery mildew on fruits and leaves.

42

drop or at a later stage the grapes may become hard and distorted and split, and are then often affected by secondary fungi, such as grey mould (see p.41), which cause extensive rotting.

Powdery mildew can be prevented to a certain extent by mulching and watering to stop the soil from drying out completely. As soon as the disease appears apply benomyl, thiophanate-methyl or triforine with bupirimate; spraying or dusting with sulphur can also be carried out. If the disease has been troublesome in previous years the first application of fungicide, whichever is used, should be given 10 to 14 days before mildew is expected. Four applications during the season may be needed to keep the disease in check. In a cold greenhouse in dull weather, it may be necessary to provide some heat temporarily so as to avoid too humid an atmosphere and careful but sufficient ventilation should be given to get good air circulation. Over-crowding of the shoots and leaves must be avoided to prevent stagnant air conditions. In a warm greenhouse the pipes can be painted with a sulphur solution but this must be done with care to avoid contact with and scorching of the lower foliage. The solution is made by mixing well equal parts of flowers of sulphur and soft soap, making lumps about the size of golf balls. One of these is put into a jam jar with a little water and stirred with the brush which is used to paint the pipes. The same mixture can be used to paint the vine stems while they are dormant in the winter, after the loose bark has been gently scraped away with a knife (see p.8).

Downy mildew occurs only occasionally in this country, mainly on outdoor grapes. It shows as light green blotches on the upper surface of the leaves and as a downy mildew on the lower surface of these patches. Affected areas dry up and become brittle causing the leaves to curl and fall. Diseased berries shrivel and become brown and leathery. The tips of the shoots may also be attacked. Remove and destroy all diseased tendrils and leaves to remove the overwintering stage of the fungus, although some spores also overwinter in the bud scales and shoots. Where infection is expected to occur, apply a protective spray of zineb, bordeaux mixture, burgundy mixture or liquid copper, *not* when the vines are in flower, and repeat at 10-14 day intervals, ceasing when further spraying would cause an unsightly spotting of the fruit. (See also Vine Blister Mite, p.39).

Honey fungus. Both indoor and outdoor vines are very susceptible to infection by this soil-borne fungus which can kill affected plants very rapidly. White fan-shaped growths of fungus develop beneath the bark of the roots and main stems at and just above ground level. Brownish black root-like structures known as rhizomorphs may be found growing on diseased roots; these grow out through the soil and spread the disease. Control of the fungus is difficult and it is essential, therefore, to trace the source of infection so that all woody debris can be dug up and burnt together with dead and dying vines and as many roots as possible. The soil should be treated with a proprietary product containing a phenolic emulsion or sterilised with a 2% solution of formaldehyde or should be changed before replanting.

Disorders

Magnesium deficiency. Vines are soon affected by a soil deficiency of magnesium, symptoms being produced in the leaves. These usually show as a yellowish orange discoloration between the veins, but in some cultivars the leaves may have purplish blotches. Later the affected areas turn brown; these symptoms should not be confused with sun scorch (p.45). The deficiency can be corrected by spraying the foliage at the first signs of trouble, with $\frac{1}{2}$lb (220g) of magnesium sulphate in $2\frac{1}{2}$ gal. (11 litres) of water plus a spreader such as soft soap or a few drops of a mild washing-up liquid. Apply two or three times at fortnightly intervals. Soil applications act more slowly, but are useful as a long-term cure. For outdoor grapes apply the magnesium sulphate in subsequent years as a soil dressing in late spring at 2 oz per sq. yd. (66g/m^2).

Spray damage. Damage by sprays, usually due to the misuse of weedkillers (such as 2,4-D; 2,4,5-T; mecoprop), occurs on both indoor and outdoor vines. Affected leaves become narrow and fan-shaped, are frequently cupped and the shoots twist spirally. Affected plants usually grow out of the symptoms in due course, but it is better to avoid such damage by the careful use of hormone weedkillers. Keep special equipment for their use, do not spray on a windy day nor use within 400 yards of outdoor grapes. Close all ventilators in greenhouses if any spraying is to be carried out in the vicinity. Do not leave weedkillers in a greenhouse as vapours from them may affect plants on a hot day.

Shanking first shows at the early ripening stage when odd berries or small groups of berries do not colour and develop naturally. It starts as a dark spot along the stalk of the grape which is finally girdled so that it shrivels and the grape stops developing and fails to ripen. The grapes are watery; black grapes turn red and white grapes remain translucent. The fruit if tasted will be found sour and unpalatable.

This disorder is usually a result of one or more unsuitable cultural conditions, such as faulty root action, due to too wet or too dry soil conditions, or the penetration of stagnant soil by the roots, or over-cropping of the vine which puts an undue strain upon the root system. The remedy, therefore is to study the soil conditions to see whether the roots could have been affected by drought or waterlogging. Mulching or resoiling may be necessary if there is any sign of such damage. At the same time reduce the crop for a year or two until the vine has regained its vigour. When shanking occurs fairly early in the season it is sometimes possible to save the rest of the crop by cutting out the withered berries and spraying the foliage with a foliar feed, providing the vine is not being

Fig. 32 (left). Shanking has occurred in the lower part of this bunch.
Fig. 33 (right). Scald shows as sunken patches on the berries.

overcropped by taking too many bunches.

Fruit splitting. This trouble most commonly occurs as a result of an attack by powdery mildew (see p.42). However it is occasionally due to irregular growth such as may occur when heavy rain follows a period of drought. Affected grapes usually rot as a result of subsequent grey mould infection. There is very little which can be done to prevent this trouble apart from mulching to conserve moisture and by watering in dry periods before the soil dries out completely.

Scald and scorch. Scald which shows as discoloured sunken patches on the berries, and scorching of the foliage which results in large pale brown patches, is due to hot sun striking through glass on to moist tissues. These troubles usually occur where the ventilation has been poor. Remove affected berries and leaves.

Oedema is a physiological disorder which is more likely to occur on vines grown under glass. Fairly late in the season, small wart-like outgrowths appear on the stalks when the fruits are developing and sometimes on the grapes themselves and even on the lower leaf surfaces. These outgrowths may break open and then have a blister-like or white powdery appearance, or they may become rusty coloured and appear as brown scaly patches. The trouble is caused when the roots of an affected plant take up more water than the leaves can transpire and this may be due to

Fig. 34. Oedema on grape berries.

extremely moist conditions either in the soil or in the atmosphere or both. Once oedema has occurred, do not remove the affected parts as this will only make the trouble worse. No special treatment can be given and the remedy is to maintain drier conditions both in the air and soil; with correct cultural treatment the affected plant should recover in due course.

Exudations. A common phenomenon in the spring is the presence of transparent globules resembling eggs, on the lower leaf surfaces and petioles. These small round greenish or colourless droplets are not the eggs of any pest but are due to a natural exudation from the plant. This type of exudation commonly occurs on young growth and indicates that the root action is very vigorous and the plant is in good health. The symptoms are inclined to be more obvious, however, on plants growing under glass where the atmosphere is humid.